I0422842

Forex Liquidity Trading

Strategies for Capitalizing on Market Movements and

Flow for making Consistent Profit

Abraham Robert. C

Copyright©2024 Abraham Robert .C

All Rights Reserved

This book comes with a link that grants you unique access to a complimentary video courses, which will enhance your trading experience by adding a visual learning elements.

FREE BONUS VIDEO COURSES

Get the access link at the end of this book

TABLE OF CONTENT

Chapter 1

Forex Liquidity

The term liquidity relates to how busy a market is. It is defined by the number of active traders and their overall trading volume.

The fact that the foreign currency market is traded 24 hours a day during the week contributes to its liquidity. It is also a tremendously deep market, with daily turnover of more than $7 trillion.

Although liquidity changes as financial centers across the world open and close during the day, there is often a large amount of forex trading going on at all times.

Liquidity Provider in Forex Market

A liquidity provider might be a market broker or an entity that functions as a professional market maker, functioning on both sides of currency transactions. Several sorts of market players add liquidity to the forex market, raising forex liquidity volume.

These include central banks, large commercial and investment banks, hedge funds, foreign investment managers, forex brokers, retail traders, and high-net-worth people. Tier 1 liquidity providers are the most prominent players in the foreign exchange market.

These comprise of the top investment banks with substantial forex departments that give buy/sell quotations for the currency pairs that they create markets in, as well as a range of additional services to its clients.

Why Should Forex Trader Care About Liquidity

Forex liquidity affects trading expenses and the efficacy of trading methods. When liquidity diminishes, trading expenses rise, affecting the outcomes of trading methods significantly. For example, scalpers require highly liquid assets to be lucrative, therefore illiquid assets are undesirable.

When fluctuating liquidity is taken into account, traders who use the same approach across all currency pairings, even if completely automated, may produce less lucrative outcomes than those who optimize.

Important Of Liquidity in Forex Trading

Faster transaction speeds

Order fill times are shortened when there is plenty of liquidity since trades can be completed swiftly. This quickness is critical for traders seeking to capitalize on short-term market fluctuations.

Reduced Slippage

In a liquid market, the actual execution price of a trade is more likely to match the expected price. This reduces slippage, which is the gap between a trade's projected price and the price at which it is actually performed.

Market Predictability

With steady liquidity, the forex market follows recognized patterns and technical indications more dependably. These patterns can help traders better predict market moves.

Strong Support and Resistance Levels

Liquidity aids in the establishment of strong support and resistance levels, which are essential for technical analysis. These levels are more dependable in a liquid market since they require a large number of deals to be breached.

Scaling opportunities

Scalping, a strategy that includes making a large number of modest returns on slight price fluctuations, thrives in the forex market due to its liquidity. Scalpers profit from fast execution and modest spreads.

Diverse Trading Strategy

High liquidity enables the employment of a variety of trading tactics, including day trading, swing trading, and position trading. Traders can select a technique that best suits their investment style and risk tolerance.

Resilience to market shocks

A liquid market can handle unexpected news or events with minimal volatility.

While important news will always have an impact, liquidity tends to mitigate excessive market fluctuations, offering some protection against wild swings.

Better Technical Analysis

Liquidity enables smoother price charts and better technical analysis. Indicators and patterns are more reliable because price action reflects true market sentiment rather than the noise of illiquid markets.

Greater Investment Flow

High liquidity draws more participants, hence increasing liquidity even further. This positive cycle stimulates more global investments, broadening and deepening the FX market.

Ease of access and exit

For traders, one of the most significant benefits of liquidity is the flexibility to enter and exit positions at any time without having to find a buyer or seller. Forex trading's appeal is largely due to its flexibility.

Tighter spreads

High liquidity is related with reduced spreads, which means that the difference between bid and ask prices is smaller. This lowers trading expenses and enables traders to enter and exit positions more economically.

Improved price stability

Liquid markets are less prone to huge, erratic price movements because the vast volume of trades absorbs individual buy and sell orders with minimal price changes. This steadiness is critical for traders who want to execute exact methods without the risk of slippage.

Enhanced Market Efficiency

Liquidity guarantees that forex market prices accurately represent all available information, since the high volume of trades allows for the speedy incorporation of news and data. This efficiency is critical to the operation of a fair and transparent market.

Easier execution of large orders

large orders can be executed more readily in a liquid market without having a significant impact on market prices.

This is significant for institutional traders and others who deal in high volumes since it allows them to trade more discreetly and efficiently.

Accessibility to All Traders

Individuals, institutions, and central banks can all trade on the forex market due to its high liquidity levels. This inclusion increases the market's energy and dynamism.

The Significance of Trading Times and Their Effect On Forex Liquidity

Despite the Forex market's continuous operation, trading periods have an impact on volume, liquidity, and price activity.

The London session is projected to account for 45% of total Forex activity, making it the key liquidity engine.

The US session is normally the second most liquid session after London, and the start of the New York session, which coincides with the last few hours of the London session, usually results in the most liquid trading time. High-frequency traders, high-volume trades, and scalpers pay special attention to these liquidity events.

The Asian session has reduced trading volumes and liquidity, resulting in range-bound markets that follow support and resistance levels established during the London session.

The Tokyo session brings the most liquidity to the Asian trading session.

Traders should focus on the opening and last trading hours of each equities trading session in global financial centers, when the majority of trading activity happens. Trading volume is typically higher in the first hour than in the latter hour of each session, with few exceptions.

How does the liquidity of a Forex pair affect the spread width

Forex trading relies on both liquidity and spread width. The spread is the difference between the purchasing (bid) price (the highest price a dealer is ready to pay) and the selling (ask) price (the lowest price a dealer is willing to accept for a currency pair). Liquidity has a direct impact on spread width: the more liquid a currency pair, the narrower the spread.

Brokers generally charge lower commissions in currency pairs with strong liquidity. It would be advantageous for traders to trade in highly liquid currency pairings in order to cut expenditures and enhance net earnings.

In highly liquid pairings, such as EUR/USD, where big financial institutions and traders are actively engaged, the spread is often tight, indicating that the difference between buying and selling Forex prices is tiny. This is helpful to traders since it lowers the cost of entering and exiting positions.

In contrast, spreads in less liquid pairs are typically greater, which can increase trading expenses. Most traders choose highly liquid currency pairings, which provide cost effective trading opportunities.

Chapter 2

Currency Pairs and Liquidity

Currency pairs on the Forex market are classified into three types: majors, minors, and exotics. Each class typically exhibits varying degrees of liquidity, with the majors accounting for the great bulk of the Forex market's trading volume, followed by the minors and finally exotics.

For example, the US dollar accounts for around 80% of all Forex deals, whilst an exotic currency like the Vietnamese dong accounts for less than 1%.

These differences have an impact on the efficacy of trading methods, risk management, and trading expenses.

Beginner traders should begin trading with the more liquid currency pairs before moving on to more advanced trading strategies for less liquid ones. As traders shift from main pairs to minor pairs and then to exotic pairings, the volume of forex liquidity decreases.

High liquidity

High market liquidity is defined by a large number of buyers and sellers, which results in high trading volumes. During these times, the difference between bid and ask prices tends to decrease, lowering slippage and transaction costs.

High liquidity also improves price stability, allowing prices to move in more manageable chunks. These could be ideal market circumstances for traders.

High liquidity in forex can also refer to a currency pair that can be purchased and sold in big quantities without experiencing significant fluctuations in its exchange rate (price level), such as major currency pairs like EUR/USD.

Other big currency (very liquid) pairs to keep an eye on

- GBP/USD

- USD/JPY

- EUR/GBP

- AUD/USD

- USD/CAD

- USD/CHF

- NZD/USD

Major currency pairs frequently have significant liquidity due to broad acceptance.

Low liquidity

In contrast, illiquidity is characterized by fewer active traders and lower trading volume. This situation frequently results in bigger bid-ask spreads, which translate to increased transaction costs for traders.

Furthermore, price swings can be volatile and unpredictable, resulting in slippage and price gaps. Exotic currency pairings that represent smaller or emerging economies, like EUR/TRY (euro/Turkish lira) or USD/ZAR (US dollar/South African rand), are frequently linked to lower liquidity.

Measuring forex liquidity

Measuring liquidity in the forex market can be challenging, primarily because there is no one exchange where all transactions take place. However, in order to evaluate the relative liquidity of a currency pair, traders frequently employ a number of indicators.

Indicators for Measuring Liquidity

• **The bid-ask spread:** is a clear measure of liquidity. A tight spread indicates high liquidity, whereas a broad spread implies poor liquidity.

• **Volume:** Strong trade volumes indicate increased liquidity, whereas low volumes indicate decreased liquidity. However, because to the FX markets decentralized nature, precise volume data might be difficult to get. To assess relative liquidity, it is preferable to compare a pair's volume to its historical volume rather than two independent pairs.

• **Price Movement:** Price changes reflect liquidity. Prices vary steadily in liquid markets, with no abrupt gaps or dramatic spikes, whereas illiquid markets are volatile and frequently produce gaps.

• **Market Depth:** Some trading platforms offer order book depth, which can provide insight into market liquidity. A large order book containing several buy and sell orders at various price levels implies great liquidity.

Forex Market Liquidity Indicators and Measures

Assessing quantitative measures is an important first step in conducting a thorough forex market liquidity analysis. Let's look at some popular indicators that may be used to analyze liquidity levels based on trading volume:

On-Balance Volume (OBV): OBV determines the strength of a price trend by examining the relationship between volume flow and price changes. Higher liquidity is often associated with stronger and more sustained price changes.

Volume Oscillator: When the volume oscillator is positive or above a certain threshold, it suggests that recent trade volume was quite high. This could indicate that there is more liquidity in the asset.

The Money Flow Index (MFI); includes trading volume in its calculations. A large trading volume, along with considerable price changes, can result in a higher MFI reading, indicating robust market involvement and possibly increased liquidity.

A lower MFI reading during price changes may be the consequence of low trading volume, which could indicate decreased liquidity and possibly decreased market interest.

Illiquidity

Illiquidity is a crucial topic to understand while trading forex. In contrast to a market with high liquidity, which is extremely active, a market with low liquidity is passive.

Illiquidity is the market's inability to transform an asset into cash fast. In forex trading, illiquidity indicates that it is difficult to enter or exit a position due to low volume (which might occur as a result of macroeconomic factors), leading the price to swing suddenly. Sometimes you may not be able to close your positions at all.

Warning Signs of Illiquidity

Using our understanding of how liquidity works in the forex market, we can begin to identify some of the warning indications of illiquidity that may indicate that it is best to avoid a position until liquidity improves.

•**Widening Spreads:** Widening bid-ask spreads are a clear symptom of illiquidity. Wide spreads are frequently seen around the end of trading sessions or soon before a major economic the announcement.

• **Increased Slippage:** Slippage occurs when a trade is executed at a different price than anticipated. If your orders are constantly being filled at unfavorable prices, you may be trading in an illiquid market.

• Price Gaps: Illiquid markets are more likely to see price gaps, which occur when a currency pair moves from one level to another without trading in between. This is due to a lack of buyers or sellers at specific price levels, which can cause prices to rise dramatically until an order is filled.

• **Higher Volatility:** Illiquid markets can see significant price changes, even with tiny deals. If you detect unpredictable and significant price movements without corresponding changes in fundamental fundamentals, it may suggest a lack of liquidity.

• **Decreased Market Depth:** A shallow order book, with fewer buy and sell orders at different price levels, indicates illiquidity. This may be particularly obvious in lesser-known or exotic currency pairs.

While EUR/USD is the most popular forex pair in terms of daily traded volume, there are several other feasible currency pairs with significant liquidity that traders can use to try to profit. Traders should consider a variety of factors before deciding on a currency pair to trade, as well as conduct their own technical and fundamental analysis to determine whether the currency pair is a viable trading option at that time, depending on central bank announcements or ongoing trade disputes.

Chapter 3

Factors Affecting Liquidity in Forex Trading

Market participants, economic events, and geopolitical developments all have an impact on liquidity in the forex market. Understanding the elements that influence liquidity in Forex trading is critical for traders since they can have a big impact on their trading tactics and profits.

Here are some of the elements affecting liquidity in Forex trading:

Market Participants:

The number and kind of market participants have a significant impact on liquidity in the forex market.

Banks, financial institutions, and retail traders are the main players in the Forex market. Banks and financial institutions are the market's major liquidity suppliers, with retail traders adding to the liquidity by placing smaller orders. The liquidity of a market increases as the number of players grows.

Economic Events

Economic events such as interest rate decisions, GDP statistics, and employment data can have a considerable impact on forex market liquidity. Economic developments can generate abrupt price movements, resulting in significant volatility and limited liquidity. For example, the release of US Non-Farm Payroll statistics might trigger a sudden increase in trade activity, resulting in lower market liquidity.

Geopolitical developments

Geopolitical factors such as political instability, wars, and natural disasters can all have an impact on Forex market liquidity. During times of crisis, traders prefer to flock to safe-haven currencies like the US dollar and the Japanese yen, resulting in less liquidity in other currencies.

Time of Day

The time of day influences liquidity in the Forex market. The foreign exchange market is open for business around the clock, five days a week, Monday to Friday. However, liquidity changes with the time of day. The European and US trading sessions have the most liquidity, while the Asian session has less liquidity.

Trading volume:

Trading volume is a primary driver of market liquidity. Higher trading volume typically suggests better liquidity because more buyers or sellers are actively participating in the market at that particular time period.

Bid/Ask spreads

The bid-ask spread is the difference between the maximum price a buyer is willing to pay (bid) and the lowest price a seller is willing to accept. Narrow bid-ask spreads suggest greater liquidity because there is less price difference between buyers and sellers. Equities with limited liquidity may have bigger spreads, increasing transaction costs for market players.

Market Depth

Market depth is the number of purchase and sell orders available at various price levels. A deep market with significant buy and sell orders improves liquidity because traders have access to a wider pool of prospective counterparties.

The Big Board, as one of the world's largest stock exchanges, normally provides deep markets for most actively traded companies. However, during moments of market volatility or low trading activity, market depth may fall, resulting in less liquidity and perhaps greater bid-ask spreads.

Market Structure

The development of electronic trading platforms and high-frequency trading (HFT) changed the market landscape. While electronic trading has boosted overall liquidity by allowing for faster and more efficient order execution, HFT may cause short-term volatility and liquidity disruptions. Market participants must comprehend and adapt to these fundamental changes in order to efficiently traverse the marketplace.

Chapter 4

Overcoming Challenges of Trading Low-Liquidity Currencies

Many traders find it difficult to trade currencies with limited liquidity. However, it is not impossible to overcome the hurdles that come with it. Taking the following step will help traders overcome the challenges of trading low liquidity currencies.

Research the currency:

Before trading a low-liquidity currency, you should thoroughly research it. This entails knowing its economic and political context, as well as determining the reasons driving price swings.

Choose the Right Broker

Trading low-liquidity currencies necessitates a broker who provides narrow spreads and consistent execution. The broker should have a thorough understanding of these currencies' intricacies and provide enough support to traders. Furthermore, traders should choose a broker that provides a variety of trading platforms, such as web-based, desktop, and mobile.

Implement proper risk management.

Trading low-liquidity currencies can be volatile, therefore it is critical to have a solid risk management strategy in place. This involves placing stop-loss orders to limit losses and employing proper position sizing.

Traders should also try diversifying their holdings to decrease their exposure to a particular currency.

Be patient

Low-liquidity currencies can be illiquid, and orders may take some time to fill. Traders should exercise patience and avoid chasing the market. It's also important to prevent overtrading, which can result in substantial losses.

Trading low-liquidity currencies can be a lucrative business if done right. Traders should thoroughly research the currency, select the best broker, practice proper risk management, and be patient.

These tactics will assist traders in overcoming the hurdles of trading low-liquidity currencies and increasing their earnings.

Approaching Forex Trading with a Liquidity Mindset

Adopting a liquidity mindset is essential when trading forex. Understanding market liquidity and staying current on market news and happenings can help traders make informed decisions and prevent surprise losses.

Important things to remember are the following

1. An asset's liquidity is determined by how simple it is to buy or sell it without changing its value. In the forex market, it relates to how easy it is to trade a particular currency pair.

Many factors influence liquidity, including economic and political stability, interest rates, and market mood.

2. Trading during high liquidity periods can help ensure that trades are completed swiftly and at a reasonable cost.

3. Keeping an eye on market news, For example, political unrest or a rapid rise in interest rates could create a major fluctuation in the currency's price.

4. A liquidity mindset is necessary, but so is a thorough understanding of technical and fundamental analysis. These tools can help traders detect prospective trading opportunities and make sound judgments.

5. Keep in mind that, like any other investment, forex trading is risky. Even with a liquidity mindset and a sound trading technique, unexpected occurrences can occur. As usual, careful risk management is vital, and you should never spend more than you can afford to lose.

Chapter 5

Understanding the liquidity pools

Liquidity Pools are critical locations in the market where there is an excess of buy and sell orders, acting as a reservoir of liquidity.

Definition and characteristics of liquidity pools

Liquidity Pools are market zones or levels where the price is likely to turn around due to an influx of orders. These zones are distinguished by a high concentration of stop-loss, take-profit, and pending orders. Recognizing these pools is critical for traders because they offer significant trading opportunities due to the high chance of price reversals or breakouts.

Impact of Institutional Order Flow

Institutional Order Flow refers to the total number of orders or transactions placed in the forex market by institutional traders. Understanding this can assist retail traders accurately identify prospective market changes and trends.

Institutional Order Flow can also be refers to the technique by which institutional traders' purchase and sell orders, these orders impact price behavior in the forex market. This effect is substantial since it has the ability to cause big market fluctuations. Knowing the direction of Institutional Order Flow enables regular traders to match their trading tactics with the market's major players, potentially resulting in more lucrative deals.

The importance of institutional order flow in determining market patterns

Understanding the directional flow of orders from institutional traders is critical since it frequently affects the direction of market moves. Institutional traders have the capital to dramatically impact the market, therefore their trading operations frequently initiate new trends or reverse existing ones. Analyzing Institutional Order Flow can help retail traders anticipate possible market swings and place their trades accordingly.

Now that we've learned about the importance and impact of Institutional Order Flow, we must grasp how to apply it to develop profitable trading strategies.

Analyze institutional order flow for effective trading techniques

Analyzing Institutional Order Flow entails examining market depth and order book data to determine the direction and volume of market orders placed by institutional investors.

Using tools and indicators like the ones listed in the previous chapters of this book can provide insights into market depth and order book data that can assist traders in detecting probable market changes based on Institutional Order Flow.

Recognizing these changes early allows traders to position their transactions strategically before large market movements occur.

With a good understanding of Liquidity Pools and Institutional Order Flow, let's look at how traders might strategically apply this knowledge.

Strategic application

Developing techniques that take into account Liquidity Pools and Institutional Order Flow is critical for trading success. To limit the risks involved, it is critical to address this with realistic examples and precautionary advice.

Developing techniques that incorporate liquidity pools and institutional order flow analysis

Developing strategies entails finding liquidity pools and monitoring institutional order flow to forecast probable market movements.

Traders can utilize market depth analysis techniques to determine where Liquidity Pools are situated and then align their trading tactics with the observed Institutional Order Flow.

This allows traders to enter trades that are in sync with market moves affected by significant market participants, boosting the likelihood that their trades will be lucrative.

Demonstrating practical use of the strategies.

To understand the actual implementation of these methods, consider the following scenario: a trader detects a Liquidity Pool with a concentration of stop-losses positioned above a resistance level. If the Institutional Order Flow appears to be bullish, the trader can place a buy order slightly above the resistance level, anticipating a breakout caused by the triggering of stop-loss orders.

In another example, if a Liquidity Pool is found near a support level with a concentration of stop-loss orders below it, and the Institutional Order Flow is bearish, a sell order might be placed slightly below the support level to anticipate a breakdown.

How Does Forex Liquidity Impact the Risk-Reward Ratio

In financial markets, risk and reward tend to rise or fall in proportion. Many Forex traders aim for a risk-reward ratio of 1:2, which means they will risk half of the amount they hope to profit on the deal. For example, if the take profit target is 40 pips above the entry point, they will set a stop loss 20 pips below it. Many traders are unaware of how Forex liquidity affects the risk-reward ratio.

Applying the risk-reward formula during high liquidity periods, which carry over to low liquidity periods, can have an influence on trading profits since spreads widen and expenses rise as liquidity decreases. This suggests that it may be advisable to enter trades early in the London or New York sessions.

In less liquid markets, volatile price movements can easily set off a trader's stop loss. It also affects their take-profit target, as a bigger spread implies positions are terminated at less-than-optimal prices.

Rewards of High Liquidity

Tight Spreads: Increased liquidity frequently results in tighter spreads, cutting transaction costs.

Price Stability: Liquid markets have less abrupt price fluctuations, making price action easier to follow.

Easy execution: In liquid markets, orders are more likely to be filled at the requested price, which is critical when trading in high volumes.

Risks of Low Liquidity

Increased Transaction Costs: In illiquid markets with broad spreads, higher transaction costs may render certain short-term strategies unprofitable.

Volatility: The increased volatility of illiquid markets can raise the chance of loss in the absence of robust risk management measures.

Slippage: Low liquidity increases the possibility that an order will be filled at a lower price than expected, lowering profitability and potentially increasing losses.

Chapter 6

Forex liquidity: A Practical Application

Understanding and utilizing liquidity is critical to success in the fast-paced world of forex trading. This chapter investigates the practical uses of forex liquidity, emphasizing its importance in trade execution, risk management, and strategy creation.

Trade Execution

Liquidity has a direct impact on trade execution, including the speed and efficiency with which orders are fulfilled. Orders in highly liquid markets are executed quickly at the correct prices, reducing slippage and assuring exact entry and exit points.

Traders may seize chances with confidence because they know their deals will be executed smoothly, even during instances of high trading volume or volatility.

Risk Management

Effective risk management uses liquidity analysis to assess and mitigate trade risks. High liquidity increases flexibility in position management, allowing traders to quickly modify their exposure in reaction to changing market conditions.

Furthermore, liquid markets provide tighter spreads, which reduce the influence of transaction costs and improve risk-adjusted returns.

Strategy Development

Liquidity play an important part in developing trading strategies. For example:

Scalping: Traders who use scalping methods profit from high liquidity since tight spreads and rapid order execution are required to capture minor price moves over short timeframes.

Trend Following: Liquidity research can help discover currency pairs with enough trading volume to allow trend-following methods.

Trading in liquid markets enhances the possibility of long-term price fluctuations, making it easier to identify and capitalize on trends.

Event Trading: During important economic announcements or geopolitical events, liquidity dynamics can change rapidly, affecting trade execution and volatility. Traders must modify their methods to efficiently navigate these liquidity variations.

Case Study: Managing Liquidity during News Events

Consider this scenario: a central bank announces an unexpected interest rate decision. This incident causes a spike in market volatility, influencing liquidity levels in several currency pairs.

Impact on liquidity: Liquidity may momentarily decline as market players respond to the news, resulting in wider spreads and more slippage.

Adaptive Strategies

Preparation: Anticipate liquidity disruptions during news events and adjust position sizing to mitigate risk.

Use of Limit Orders: Using limit orders at key levels to enter or exit trades at targeted prices, reducing the influence of liquidity swings.

Monitoring Market Depth: Constantly watch market depth to assess liquidity conditions and adapt trading methods accordingly.

Conclusion

Forex liquidity is a critical component of trading that affects transaction execution, risk management, and strategy creation. Traders can improve their performance and confidently adjust to shifting market conditions by studying and incorporating liquidity dynamics into their trading strategy. The effective use of liquidity analysis allows traders to optimize their trading methods and capitalize on opportunities in the volatile forex market.

Video Access link

subscribepage.io/freeforexcourse

www.ingramcontent.com/pod-product-compliance
Lightning Source LLC
Chambersburg PA
CBHW070439290526
45791CB00005B/2038